KANBAN
FOR BEGINNERS

Basics about the use of Kanban in industry and software development

How Kanban Works in Practice

by Franz Millweber

Copyright and legal notice

Table of Contents

1. Introduction

Both in industrial manufacturing and in software development, production cycles are getting shorter and shorter, quality requirements are getting higher and resources are getting scarcer. In addition, there is an environment that could not be more uncertain. Even small and medium-sized businesses can already feel how quickly new technologies and management methods are conquering and transforming entire industries. Software development has always been a field in which teams have worked closely together. All the more surprising, then, that a technology that can be described as the mother of all agile methods comes from the automotive industry of all places: Kanban.

In this book you will learn what Kanban means, how to use it, where it makes sense and where it doesn't. Like many other approaches, whether in Agile or in classic waterfall project management, Kanban is not a miracle weapon and has its limits. Some of them are shown to you in this book. All you need to learn Kanban is this book, a little time and the desire to try something new. You don't even need software; you can even try Kanban on a drawing pad or on your living room wall.

The book first gives you an overview of the essential basics of Kanban and the most important terms, so that you can develop an understanding of the underlying principle of the most even workflow possible. Then we introduce you to the most important tools you use in Kanban, the board and the cards. Finally, we will briefly discuss Kanban in industrial production and show a few applications in which Kanban can still be used.

To give you an idea of what Kanban means in a few words, here is the compact form:

> In **Kanban**, work flows along a clear column model from To-Do to Doing to Done, where the columns have limitations on the number of tasks. In addition, the tasks are not pushed but fetched.

In this book we have put the emphasis on software development, but in the examples we will always briefly address other areas, if only because it is sometimes a little more descriptive.

2. What does Kanban mean?

Once upon a time, Taiichi Ohno, an employee of the car manufacturer Toyota, thought about how he could improve the efficiency of car production. In Japanese, the term Kanban simply means "card". Ohno developed a system in which each production part was given a card. This card indicated which part it was, and mostly still an inventory number and the indication where it was to be found. But more important were two other codes: The minimum and maximum quantity of this part, which must be available, and the information when a new order must be triggered.

One of the problems with car manufacturers and their suppliers was the estimation of the production quantity. In most cases, planning and production was done months in advance. If the demand for cars was too low, the department stores overflowed; if they were too large, important parts were missing to produce enough cars.

With the Kanban cards, a system was introduced that ensured that there were only as many elements in the warehouse as were needed. Ohno was primarily concerned with avoiding overcapacities. This also gave rise to the terms "work in progress" and "just in time": The work being done determined which resources were needed.

While Kanban quickly found its way into the entire automotive industry and soon into other industries, the software industry recognized the potential quite late, especially because it was assumed that there were no goods that caused overcapacities. If, however, one understands work and tickets as goods, then Kanban can also be used in software development. It's easy to see that lean manufacturing can also work in programming. Kanban offers the possibility to balance capacity and demand quite well and at the same time to eliminate the often existing bottlenecks.

The breakthrough came in 2010 with a book by David Anderson describing how he developed Kanban from a project at Microsoft. The decisive factor for the software was not so much the danger of overcapacity as the pull system. The developers were no longer given work but were able to get it themselves depending on their capacities. The work in progress in this case was not machines that needed screws for car doors but designers and developers who worked on software. At the same time, Scrum came up, a system similar to Kanban but with differences. The developer Corey Ladas tried to combine both approaches in his book, *Scrumban*, which then led to different other hybrid forms.

Today Kanban is above all a way to visualize a process and to accelerate it through the associated transparency and to quickly eliminate bottlenecks. At Kanban, the main thing is to work continuously and avoid interruptions and delays. The focus is on the customer and his needs, which have to be fulfilled.

The focus is on the Kanban board, a board on which the entire process is visualized. Especially in smaller teams and companies, a board is really used for this, around which people gather in the morning and discuss the next steps. Visualization is an important basis at Kanban, no matter if it is realized electronically or physically. The simplest form consists of three columns. The first column contains the work that has to be done, the second column contains everything that is in progress and the third column contains the work that can be delivered.

2.1 Kaizen

Kanban is often used in large companies where a Kaizen philosophy has already been implemented. The word comes from Japanese and originally means "change for the better". In Japan, this has become a principle of corporate governance and production. You don't assume that you have to wait for an innovation and then use all your resources to bring it to market. Rather, the focus is on a continuous process of improvement. This is based on the principle of giving the customer the best possible product. The improvement takes place at all levels of an organization. Important points at Kaizen are:

- An open internal suggestion system

- Employee management

- Process orientation

- Quality management

It is also important to understand the Kaizen way of thinking. It is fundamentally different from traditional companies, which are essentially profit-oriented and want to save costs. Kaizen has different priorities. An organization needs to focus on the following:

Processes: The focus is not on the result but on the process that leads to it.

Customers: Products must satisfy the customer and give him added value.

Quality: Products and services must be of the highest quality that can be achieved. Quality must therefore be constantly monitored.

Criticism: Innovations and improvements come only through a discourse within the workforce. This is why an open collaboration structure and an open suggestion system are needed.

Standards: Learning from mistakes also means introducing the improvements you make as new standards so that mistakes are avoided in the future.

If you want to introduce Kanban, it doesn't hurt to familiarize yourself with Kaizen. Companies that internalize the essential way of thinking of Kaizen will find it easier to introduce methods like Kanban but also Scrum and other agile development environments.

At Kaizen, the product is continuously improved and one way is to identify and eliminate bottlenecks. Kanban was also derived from this because the bottleneck was the biggest problem in warehousing. But also in the daily development there can be such bottlenecks. From the bottleneck theory you can use the following solutions, which are also part of the Kaizen philosophy:

- Identify the bottleneck

- Fully utilise this area

- Ensure that the following and upstream processes are oriented to the bottleneck

- Fix the bottleneck

You can use a traffic jam caused by a construction site as a picture. The first thing you notice is that there is a traffic jam because of the construction site. Then you try to change the construction site so that as many cars as possible get through. At the same time, you use warning signals to try to slow down the traffic by 10 kilometres before the construction site so that fewer cars pass the construction site at the same time. Then you try to get the construction site finished as quickly as possible so that the traffic can flow again as usual.

Solving problems

Kaizen and Kanban try not only to solve problems but also to identify the cause. If a problem cannot be solved further, then it is necessary to investigate why the problem arose until this question has been sufficiently clarified. The 5 W system is helpful in this so-called root analysis. Five "why" questions are asked to ensure that one is not satisfied with the first answer. A classic and vivid example is late arrival. Let's say you got to the office too late.

1. Why are you late? Because I got stuck in traffic.

2. Why did you get stuck in traffic? Because I left too late.

3. Why did you leave too late? Because I overslept.

4. Why did you oversleep? Because I went to bed too late.

5. Why did you go to bed too late? Because I worked for a long time.

Only so you come in this case to the true reason for your late coming. In the industry the 5 W method is used today with many problems, in addition with large accidents and losses of production. In software development, you can use it to find out why a bug occurred and whether it was just a small bug or whether there is a malfunction in the system.

2.2 Kanban in industrial production

Kanban actually comes from production and is still used most of the time. They wanted to solve the problem that in a production process often too many parts are lying around in the department store and there are no parts at other places. This can paralyze production or even bring it to a standstill. The aim of the Kanban system was to ensure that only as many parts are produced as are actually needed while at the same time ensuring that there are always enough parts available.

This could be achieved with a quite simple means: the Kanban card. It is included with all parts. Let's assume that small loudspeaker boxes are produced at one workstation. It takes the cabinets, electronics, the speaker itself and of course a soldering station to assemble it all. Every part that is needed can be taken out of a box containing a Kanban card. Depending on the regulations, this card can be placed on the floor or, for example, on the third last part. The card indicates which part it is, how many parts are in a box, how many parts must be at least in the box. In the case of goods with a best-before date, this can also be noted. If the person at work sees the card, they give it to the warehouse or the manufacturer of the required parts. The manufacturer then refills the box accordingly.

This technology is so successful in production because, on the one hand, it ensures the smooth delivery of production equipment and, on the other, it also prevents overproduction. Just In Time (JIT) is produced, i.e. only when a card is delivered and it is clear that the parts are needed.

Even if the principle of the cards may sound a bit analogous, they are a simple and effective means of keeping the warehouse and the delivery up to date. Today, many cards still have barcodes that usually describe the product packed in a container.

Kanban cards also track a complete product or order. Let's say your company has received an order for 300 speakers. This order is placed on a Kanban card attached to a container containing 300 containers. It is located at the end of the production line. When the 300 loudspeakers are finished, he moves with the card to the packaging and from there to the shipping company. This is where the barcodes come into their own because when the container is in the truck at the latest, you no longer have access to the card. When the container is delivered, the Kanban card is scanned and the process is completed. Usually this message is then passed on to the accounting department, which can then issue an invoice.

One example is Georg Fischer AG, a supplier to the automotive industry. The company produces heavy-duty cast parts for car manufacturers all over the world. Production is therefore carried out in Germany, Austria and China. The company's foundry must, of course, be as busy as possible so that it is profitable. However, orders do not come in daily. This means that, in addition to capacity utilisation, overproduction must also be considered. Until now, classic planning has consisted of management trying to set a realistic target and then producing to that target. However, this repeatedly led to production bottlenecks and overproduction.

The Kanban boards were introduced in the foundry, which represented the current status of the respective production. Kanban boards are inserted into these boards, which in turn indicate where a part is located within a process. In concrete terms, this looks like this:

"The semi-finished products of the foundry are stored in defined containers. As soon as a container is filled, it is provided with an appropriately labelled kanban card and moves to the processing department. This means that the card is missing from the control panel.

As soon as the downstream production island has further processed all semi-finished products and the container is empty, the card returns to one of the compartments on the board. So when there is no card left on the control panel, all the containers are in circulation." [1]

The Kanban boards serve on the one hand as an overview and help with planning, and on the other hand they also indicate the levels of urgency. The Kanban boards also have another advantage: they force employees from different departments to gather in front of them and discuss together how production is going, whether there are any problems and how these can be solved.

---

[1] Weigand: Die Kanban Methode in der Praxis. URL: https://www.weigang.de/de/themenwelt/methoden/kanban/kanban-anwendungsbeispiel [as of: 20-08-2018]

3. Kanban in software development

Today Kanban is also used in software development and general project management, albeit in a slightly modified form. Since most projects are not so much about avoiding overcapacities in the warehouse, Kanban focuses on the flow. While in industry the cards are the most important; in other projects it is the board that gives an overview of the current status. Kanban is seen as a new way to develop products quickly and efficiently.

We owe the use of Kanban in IT to David Anderson. Anderson came into contact with agile development methods back in 1997 when he was working on a project for a bank in Singapore. In 2005, he developed the first concept of agile development for Microsoft. His 2003 book, *Agile Management for Software Engineering - Applying the Theory of Constraints for Business Results*, and its successor *Kanban: Successful Evolutionary Change for Your Technology Business* were the founders of Kanban in the IT industry. Today Anderson is a Kanban trainer and helps companies use Kanban for projects.

3.1 For what and for what not

When choosing project management systems, you should always keep the goal in mind and consider how best to achieve it. Kanban can be a big help in some cases and can be a completely wrong choice in others.

Kanban is the best:

- If your company has already established certain roles and wants to keep them to a large extent.

- If you want to develop things quickly and have them prioritized.

- If you want a good overview of progress and current status at all times.

- If you want to have a holistic overview that also includes the work of suppliers or external forces.

- If you are looking for a simple method that needs little explanation and is understood by everyone.

- If you want to get by with as few rules as possible.

- If you have a team that enjoys working together and is able to organise itself.

Kanban is not suitable if:

- The work cannot be divided into small pieces

- Hierarchical decision-making structures are in place

- It should be used as a framework

- Work in waves is coming

- It is a matter of designing a project

Kanban's focus is on getting work done quickly and with high quality. It's very close to Getting Things Done, so it wants the job done. That's why it doesn't have formal loops like those found in many other systems like Scrum.

Kanban quickly reaches its limits in software development when it comes to scaling. The bigger and above all the more complex a project, the more difficult it becomes to represent this in Kanban. Either you will have to divide it into several smaller Kanban boards and projects, or you will have to look for another project management system. An exact size, from when Kanban is no longer sufficient, cannot be given. As a rule of thumb: as long as it is only about keeping things flowing and doing about 30–40 tasks at the same time, a Kanban board should still work.

The Kanban pioneer Klaus Leopold has created so-called **flight levels**, which represent where Kanban can be used in a company. [2]

Level 1: Teams have easy access that is not controlled. There is a danger of being overtaxed.

Level 2: Teams have a controlled inflow to the system and only get as much work as the team can handle. The problem here is that teams in a company also work across projects and cannot be isolated.

Level 3: The focus here is not on the team but on value creation. The goal is to optimise the added value; therefore, Kanban is also used in several teams within the organization.

---

[2] Leopold, K. (2017): Flight Level: The Organizational Improvement Levels. URL: https://www.leanability.com/en/blog-en/2017/04/flight-levels-the-organizational-improvement-levels [as of: 10-08-2018]

Level 4: This is where Kanban is used in the portfolio, as several value chains throughout the company are affected and must be integrated into the process. This level is more likely to be found in strategy departments and senior management.

You can already see from this that Kanban is versatile and is not limited to one team or project but can also take over a complete company.

3.2 Differences between Scrum and Kanban

Both Kanban and Scrum are agile methods, which differ from the classical planning office focused project methods. Often Kanban is understood as a kind of meta-level of Scrum, but this is wrong. Scrum has a similar approach, but a different methodology than Kanban.

Planning

At Scrum a lot has to be planned, and also in the implementation there are constant plans. The sprints are particularly very planning intensive. Kanban does not know such sprints. There is only work that has to be done and work that is being done (and work done). Time does not matter (at first), but the amount of work that is being done does.

Iterations

An essential part of Scrum are the iterations to ensure that there is continuous improvement. At Kanban, the flow is one-way, but that doesn't mean there are no improvements. Only these are achieved through feedback meetings. If there are problems with a software component, it remains a work in progress until the problem is solved. Until then, no further work can be accepted (unless other work is done).

Roles

At Scrum there are few but very essential roles: The Scrum master and the product owner. Without these roles, Scrum doesn't work, because they are important in decision-making processes, especially when it comes to which work has priority. At Kanban, there are no fixed roles at all, rather collaboration is the key. In practice, however, it has become established that at least one kind of project manager is needed who also has decision-making authority if no solution can be found together.

Constant Flow at Kanban

At Scrum the sprints are processed and then started again. With Kanban, this form of reset does not exist. Instead, new work is constantly fetched from the pool as long as the Work in Progress Limit has not been reached.

3.3 Scrumban

In most cases, where Agile is used today, mixed forms from different approaches are used. One has proven to be particularly good because it has the advantages of both systems, but without having major disadvantages: Scrumban is, as the name suggests, a combination of Scrum and Kanban. The main advantage is that you can combine the fast development cycles of Scrum with the good overall view of Kanban. It is more a management framework than a concrete development environment. There is no Bible for Scrumban, and you don't even know who invented it. Probably the name was dropped at a conference, also because it is obvious to connect the two systems with each other. Although there is no rulebook, a few basic concepts have been established that combine the two approaches.

Iterations

One of the special elements in Scrum are the short iterations in which a product is developed. These usually last only one or two weeks. They are also maintained in Scrumban.

Planning on demand

An essential difference to the pure Scrum is the demand-oriented processing of tasks. Here the Kanban elements come to the fore: Something is only taken from the backlog when the capacities for it have become available again. In concrete terms, this means that the development team makes use of the backlog and is not assigned its tasks by the product owner.

Board

Also Scrum knows a board, but the one from Kanban gives a better overall view. In the simple version there are the three classic columns, "To Do, Doing and Done." Here the tasks are planned and written into the first column; then limits are set for the To-Do and the Doing or Work-in-Progress column. In Scrumban the employee component is added, the rule is that an employee should only work on one task at a time.

Roles

In Scrumban there are no roles, but the work is distributed according to the respective skills, i.e. to designers, developers and testers. There is no Scrum master and no product owner' the teams are given more responsibility to organize themselves.

Meetings

Since the Daily-Scrum and the morning meeting are actually identical in both systems, there is no need for a change. You can even hold meetings every two days, but you should keep the 15-minute rule.

3.4 Kanban in game development

Game developers have always had special requirements because the way a game is produced differs from software. First of all, the planning phase takes much longer than with classic software, and, secondly, the production is very simply structured. In a game, it's normal to plan the course of the game for over a year, develop characters and invent the complete game system. Mostly you work with simple representations and only at a later point in time do you get a real workflow.

Once the planning phase or pre-production is complete, the developers and designers can go about the actual work. In contrast to software, where you often break new ground and have to test a lot, game development is mainly carried out. Therefore the classical Scrum approaches make little sense there and Kanban comes fully to the fore here. Game developers often complain that their work is similar to that of a factory worker, and you can agree with that: That's exactly why Kanban is so good because it comes from industrial production.

The boards in game development differ a little from those in software development. One form, the Heijunka board, has been particularly successful. It has the following columns:

Not Started	Script	Concert Art	Level Design	High Res Art	Auto Design	Tuning Pass	Done

Instead of a ticket the different levels are entered into the board. It is important that you follow very closely how fast the development works within the different levels. Also here it is important to have a good flow of work and therefore reduce the number of levels. However, it may take less time to write the script for level 5 than to create the high-res version for it. This can lead to a traffic jam in the end. Probably the levels will be subdivided into smaller tasks, which will then be developed in Scrum-Sprint-like cycles, especially when it comes to coding. Again, Kanban is a good instrument to overview the whole project and to see if all areas are optimally utilised.

4. The basics

In Kanban, there are only a few principles that are of a more general nature. So you won't have to deal with a long list of instructions and special terms, as is often the case with other project management systems.

4.1 The core values

In software development, some values that form the basis of this system have prevailed in the use of Kanban. They determine the framework in which KANBAN is used and are intended to provide orientation for the employees and team members involved. They are also partly based on Kaizen.

Transparency
The team members see transparency as an important basis for open communication. It is agreed that sharing knowledge facilitates and improves work for all. This also means communicating clearly and unambiguously with others.

Balance
A balance must be struck between the different views, capacities and abilities in order to be able to work

together. If the balance is lost, it can have an impact on productivity and the company.

Collaboration

In a Kanban project, everyone works together to bring the project to a successful conclusion.

Customer focus

The product being developed should and must satisfy the customer. Therefore, all activities must be oriented towards what can benefit the customer. A customer can also be another department in Kanban.

Flow

Kanban is about keeping work flowing. This is a core statement and every employee is called upon to ensure and internalize this flow.

Leadership

Kanban is led by setting a good example, inspiring others and being able to reflect. Leadership is important in Kanban to maintain the flow, but also to improve it.

Understanding

Kanban employees need to understand what knowledge and skills they have and how best to bring them into the process.

Consistency

In a Kanban process, you do not look for the conflict, but for a solution in agreement with others. We work together, which also means that different opinions and views have to be heard. The end result is not consensus, but the best solution.

Respect

Kanban employees have respect for each other. They understand and accept their team members as they are, and understand this respect as a foundation of cooperation.

4.2 Visualizing

Kanban is already a very visual method due to its origin. In production, even in a high-tech company, real cards are still used today that are put into small drawers. In software development, too, the project should definitely be visualised. This is usually done in the form of a flow diagram, which shows which area is the concept phase, what makes up the Work in Progress, and how the finished parts are processed.

For example, this can look very simplified:

The difference to a normal flowchart lies in the key figures that are built-in. One is the determination between customer and developer when a concept can be implemented. It is the interface between the concept phase and the Work in Progress (WiP). In Kanban, these are rules that are also attached to the board itself. They are visible for everyone. Also at the end of the WiP is the definition that now the product or its part can be delivered.

In addition, limits are set for the Kanban visualizations. In a WiP only a certain number of product parts can be in work at the same time. New parts can only be started once the limit has been reached. There are also time limits for the individual parts.

Because Kanban also works with many colors and symbols, you can see at a glance whether limits are exceeded, much faster than if you had to start software. With a simple Kanban board, the limit is simply a horizontal line in a column. Beyond that, you can't stick a ticket on. Everyone can see immediately whether a column is full or not.

Conceptualization, work in progress and delivery must take place within specified time periods (the time in the WiP phase is also referred to as system lead time). Accordingly, the delivery rate must also be visualized. It is calculated by dividing the "Work in Progress" parts by the "Lead Time". In order to be able to represent this even better, the "Time in Progress" unit is often used, which indicates how long a product part is in development. For such data Kanban provides as software mostly its own analysis tools. However, the distribution of the tickets and a possible clustering already indicates very well whether bottlenecks or overcapacities exist.

After all, the flow is not only displayed but also actually takes place, in which elements are repeatedly moved from left to right. In general, this is one of the most important features of Kanban: Everything is visible, be it electronically or with blackboards. And: It must be visible for everyone. Each company can decide for itself how to organize and structure the Kanban boards, as long as the basic rules are followed. Especially in software development you will sometimes reach the limits of a board. Therefore it is better to consider right at the beginning whether the project can be divided into smaller parts, which then get their own board. However, you will have to make sure that the individual boards and processes do not compete with each other and consume too many resources.

The easiest way to create a Kanban board is to record three columns: The first column is called "To-Do", the second "In Progress" and the third "Delivered". Of course you can choose the names freely; the only important thing is to keep the basic idea. The middle column is reserved for the actual work. The third column is in any case reserved for finished work.

4.3 Reducing the amount of work in progress

Kanban provides a quite simple but effective method to reduce Work in Progress. It's not about doing less work but about not working on too many things in your project at the same time. All columns in Kanban have a maximum and sometimes a minimum quantity. It doesn't matter if a container should be filled or if parts of the software should be developed. Like everything else, the amount of work that has been started must also be visualized. Usually you simply write a number at the bottom of the WiP column indicating how many individual tasks are allowed at the same time.

This is based on the pull system, in which new jobs are only accepted when enough others have been processed. This means that the developers get the respective parts of the software from the descriptions if they have free capacities. In classical project management, a plan is created for what needs to be done, and then often a mountain of work is simply presented to the team (push). With Kanban, a new work is automatically drawn when space has become available in the Work in Progress column (pull).

Restrictively there are still priorities. Some Kanban boards define the priorities in a board; others create a separate board for each priority. It is important to keep an eye on which resources are used. It is usually better to keep an eye on everything and to set rules for when which priorities are processed.

Since, apart from priorities, employees are free to decide what they want to do next in the first column, there is a risk of imbalance. As a project leader, you will need to make sure that there aren't some developers who grab the easy tasks and others who have a higher workload. It's best to discuss what's going to happen next in morning board meetings.

4.4 Keeping the flow

In Kanban everything has to flow, it's like a little canal they built. What you don't need now are beavers that build a dam or somehow block the river. You want – to stay in the picture – the water to bubble out of the spring, flow along the canal and finally end up in the sea.

In software development, beavers are often stakeholders who want to intervene in the process, but they are also misconceptions about the time a job takes. And this time is also an important unit for determining how well the work flows in the Kanban system. Time is money, as you know, and it's quite easy to show how high the cost of delays is. You give each job a certain value, and the more it is delayed, the more value is lost.

In Kanban there are four types of cost increases due to delays:

Acceleration: Costs suddenly skyrocket

Fixed date: If a work is not completed on a certain date, the costs increase to a certain level (for example, in the case of contractual penalties for non-delivery)

Standard: An almost linear curve that offsets costs against time

Indescribable: When cost increases occur due to delays, but you don't know when

As described before, Lead Time is a good indicator of how well the project is flowing. In order to solve problems you should always consider

- What does the customer expect?

- Can the system do it?

- What is agreed with the customer?

- What can I not present to the customer in any case?

4.5 Clear rules

Where many people work together, you need a few rules that set the framework in which you operate. This framework is determined by rules. However, the rules are not created by a team leader, but together, before the Kanban project starts. It is important that it is clear to you and everyone in the team that the rules must be adhered to. If the rule says that only 10 jobs can be done simultaneously, then not one person in the team can decide to take another eleventh job that can be done quickly.

The rules must be clear, and you will have to make sure that everyone understands them. Often this is also a question of language and especially with international teams it is better to ask again or even ask how someone has understood a rule.

Nevertheless, it will happen that rules are changed. Kanban is a project in flux and it can always happen that someone has a suggestion for improvement. But also for this there is a rule for how this can be discussed and implemented if you like it. So it can be that 10 jobs, which should be done at the same time, mean too much work, and you have to reduce the limit. Sometimes it also happens that work is carried out too quickly and the customer does not comply at all with accepting the individual program parts, thus creating a traffic jam at the end of the process.

The different steps in Kanban also have different rules. It is common that the respective rules are also placed either above or below the columns and are visible for everyone. Because there is little space there, you should always keep the rules short and clear. Nobody has the time and the desire to read through 10 pages.

A problem especially in software development is the definition of Done: When is a product part developed to the point that it can be presented to the customer (or is being further developed)? In Kanban you will need several such definitions at once because you also have several columns: So you will have to define when a design is finished, when a code is finished, and when a test is finished. But you will also have to define at the beginning when and under what conditions tasks can be taken from the to-do column. As with most other development methods, the definition of Done should be clear and unambiguous.

For the development of a program part this can look like this:

O Code ready, with comments and executable

O Code has been verified by others

O Code has no known errors

O Remaining time expenditure is 0 or positive

If all fields are checked, the ticket can be passed on. In KANBAN, the definition of Done must be defined for each column but also for sub-columns.

4.6 Integrating feedback

Kanban is not only a fluid method, but it also produces whirlpools, the feedback loops. In Kanban, you need constant feedback that confirms processes or identifies errors and problems that need to be solved together. With Kanban you don't write down a process and wait for what comes out at the end. Rather, it is like a machine that you monitor, that has to be lubricated and where you have to turn a screw here and there to keep everything running.

Feedback can also be institutionalized in Kanban, there are the so-called cadences. These are regular meetings where the status is discussed. Here you will have to make sure that the time periods between meetings are correct. They shouldn't be too frequent because you don't want to disturb the flow. Most of the time, it also depends on the area being studied. Strategic reviews don't take place as often as development team meetings. However, everyone involved in implementation should meet briefly every day to discuss whether there are problems and which elements have priority. Some companies also have a daily meeting for the completed work, but that usually depends on the size of the project and the company. The smaller a company, the less formal meetings you should have.

4.7 Better cooperation

At Kanban, more than with other project management methods and processes, you will need to work closely with other team members. Kanban sees the team as those who work together to ensure the flow. This is only possible together, even if there may be a team leader who has the authority to make certain critical decisions. Collaboration means that you conceptualize and define the work together, decide together what will be done next and solve any difficulties together.

A Kanbank card is also not a table carved in stone, but rather it is intended to help continuously improve a process and a project. This is precisely why there are morning Kanban meetings. It is quite common for the Kanban board to look completely different at the end of a project than it did at the planning stage. Projects develop in Kanban; that's what's wanted and what makes the method so successful.

5. Working with Kanban

At Kanban there are two important tools: The Kanban Board and the Kanban Cards. Both are actually used in industrial production but have also found their way into the software industry.

5.1 Kanban boards

A Kanban board is first of all only a board with several columns. The simplest form is three columns, but most of the time at least five columns are used today because of the different kinds of work. The first and the last column are almost all the same. The first column lists the work that must be done and the last column the work that can be delivered.

A board can look different, it can be a partition used as a blackboard or a whiteboard. In the concept phase you can still work with markers; later you will have to organise it a little better. Clearly drawn lines will help here.

Still, such boards are installed in most companies that use Kanban. In the last chapter you will also get to know software with which Kanban boards can be managed and analyzed. But especially at the beginning it is recommended to use a real board because it is a place where the team members can meet and discuss (even if limited in time). You will be able to concentrate on the essentials much more easily, namely the tickets and tasks, and will not have to learn how a software works first. Finally, a two-meter wall is still easier to visually capture than 300 tickets on a small computer monitor. Our brain can process visual information much faster than pure text. Since the Kanban Board looks like a picture to us, we can understand it better and get an overview.

If you also use colors, you will be able to make the board even clearer. Here is an example of how to work with colors:

To-Do	Planning	Development	Test	Done

The different colors represent different service classes (see below), which you can assign freely. But you will already see from this graphic that there are very few blue tickets in the test area, so there are free capacities here.

If you enter "Kanban Board" in the picture search on Google, you will see how great the variety can be: It ranges from a small three-column board to meter-long walls that occupy an entire room.

If you insist on having everything digital, you can also use a projector to throw the board against the wall. This is convenient for meetings and can save you space. However, it also has disadvantages because it's not always visible.

Sub-columns for Kanban

It is possible to subdivide the columns again in KANBAN. This is particularly useful in the Work in Progress area. Here the columns Design, Development and Testing are often subdivided into two sub-columns: "In Progress" and "Done". On the one hand, this gives you an even better overview of how far the individual WiP elements are, but on the other hand it also gives the team a better and faster overview of which parts can be transferred to Done. The pull process in the last column is one of the weaknesses of Kanban because it is often not immediately clear which tickets are already finished and can be removed. If you don't work with sub-columns, you should always add a big symbol to finished tickets, for example a green hook.

Swimlanes

Sometimes you can't bring everything into a three-column structure but need to make distinctions. This is where the so-called Swimlanes come into play. With them you interrupt the Kanban Board horizontally. Especially in the area of Work in Progress this can be helpful if things are done at the same time but by other teams. Let's say you're working on updating software that's being written and tested at the same time. If you don't want to wait until tickets in coding are finished and submitted to testing, you can also add a subboard that shares the Done column with the main board. Something like this might look like this:

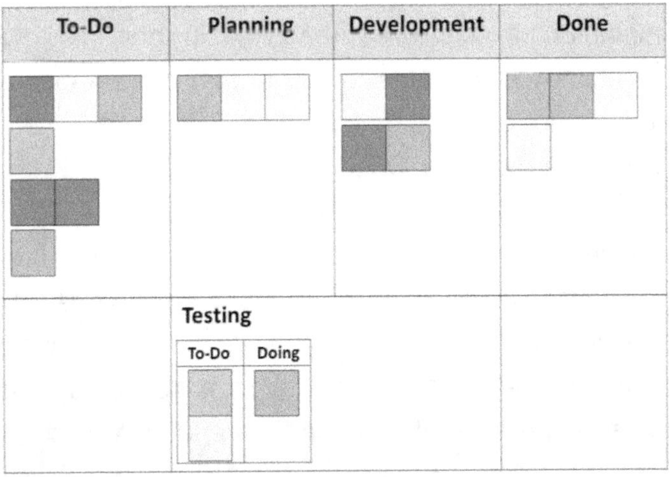

To-Do	Planning	Development	Done

Testing

To-Do	Doing

In this case, the test team has its own board but still has the overall view you and can see how far the project has progressed.

Another example is marketing. Here Kanban can be used to implement a new campaign. But such campaigns today have different channels, for example TV, digital, print, social networks. These can all be built into their own swimlanes because they are usually not interdependent. At Leankit[3] you can see many other suggestions for how boards can look, depending on how they should be used.

The Swimlanes can also be used if you have teams that are so specialized that they always work together. In this case, each team gets its own swimlane or sub-table, which in turn can be divided into further columns, for example Doing and Done or Ready, in Progress, Done.

These Swimlanes can be very practical but also tempting: If you open too many subboards, the system quickly becomes confusing and takes Kanban one of its main uses. Always try to make the board as clear as possible. If you need more than 20 seconds

____

[3] Leankit Inc.: 10 Kanban Board Example. URL: https://leankit.com/learn/kanban/kanban-board-examples-for-development-and-operations [as of: 05-08-2018]

to find or understand something then the board is probably too complicated.

Goals

Some project managers also want to make the goals they have set visible and create a separate column for them. This can be especially useful if you have set intermediate goals. Then you can add a column to the right or left of the board that shows such goals. However, they should not refer to a specific task but be formulated more comprehensively. But: they must also be concrete. It doesn't help to write that you want to be more productive. It is better to formulate the goal with "20 percent productivity increase."

Stories

In many projects the tasks are also called stories. They are listed in the To-Do column, preferably sorted by priority. The most important task should always be at the top.

Under discussion...

... it can happen that there are tasks where problems occur and which are not processed any further. Normally, a blocker would be inserted to indicate that the task is suspended and not included in the maximum number. You can also move these blocked tasks to a separate column called blocked or in discussion. Here everyone can immediately see that there is a problem and start working on the solution. Once the problem is solved, the task moves back to the To-Do list (Not in Doing).

Test

Especially in software development, a lot of testing has to be done and it makes sense if testing gets its own column. As already mentioned, the test column can also be subdivided into currently testing and finished. This makes it easier to see which tests are already finished, but you also have a better overview of how testing develops overall and whether traffic jams occur.

More variations for software developers can be found here: [4]

https://www.sitepoint.com/how-why-to-use-the-kanban-methodology-for-software-development/

And another tip: A board should not be carved in stone. If you feel that something should be changed as the project progresses, talk to your team about it. In such cases, there are various meetings, including the strategy meeting.

---

[4] Laptick, S. (2016): How & Why to Use the Kanban Methodology for Software Development.URL; https://www.sitepoint.com/how-why-to-use-the-kanban-methodology-for-software-development/ [as of: 22-07-2018]

5.2 Kanban cards

In industrial production, plastic cards are mostly used, which are printed, or in material management a cardboard box with appropriate imprint. Today there are already manufacturers of Kanban boards and cards, even with drawers and in different colours. But if you want to try out Kanban or if there are many changes typical for software development, then you are best served with a large and long whiteboard with small stickers.

The design of the cards or tickets is up to you, but it's important that there's as little information on it as possible. A classic Kanban card in software development looks like this:

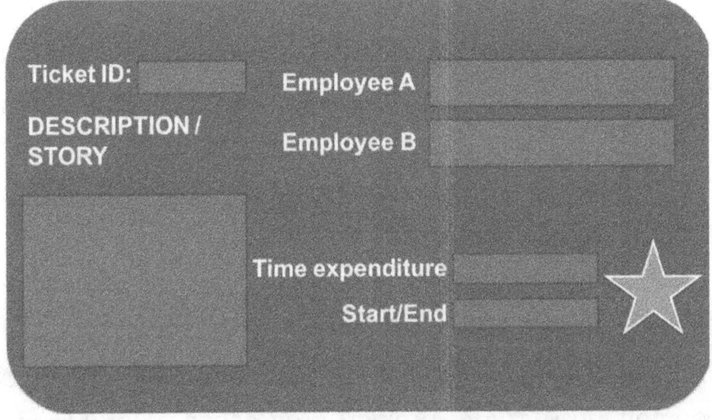

The most important information on a map is:

- Title of the task

- Ticket ID

- Service class (can also be represented by colors)

- Times (start/end)

- Related activities or people (if other developers need to work on them as well)

- Skill-Levels (what you have to know to complete the task)

- Urgencies

- Blocker symbol (in the above case the asterisk)

In the planning phase it is important to talk about the layout of the maps and to build a prototype. If the time is available, you should do some trial runs with this prototype. These will show whether you need more, less or other information on the map. Then you can print a first batch of cards, preferably on a slightly firmer paper. But don't print 1000 cards at once because you'll find that you need to change something as the project progresses. Hardly any

Kanban project has ever been completed in the same way as it started.

You can see again and again that Kanban uses Post-It stickers. In the initial phase, especially when it comes to planning the Kanban board and the individual elements, these also work. The practical thing is that you can get them in several sizes and colors. Later, however, it becomes very tedious to label them, especially if cards are to have certain conventions. Also, the adhesive strength of a sticker has its limits, and you have better things to do than pick up dropped tickets and see where they belong. The more extensive and long-term the project, the more likely you are to want to print your own tickets.

5.2.1 Tracking

As long as the number of tasks and tasks in progress can be seen at a glance, you should have no problems seeing the flow. But as soon as it becomes more complex and you work with different swimlanes, it can quickly become confusing. While you will still be able to visually see if there is a bottleneck or idle, when it comes to finding a particular ticket, it can take some time. That's why Porsche has bar-coded all its tickets. This barcode contains all the information about the ticket. Each column on the board then receives a small barcode scanner. If a ticket was moved, it was also pulled over the barcode scanner and checked into the respective column. But it is a little bit easier to provide the tickets with a QR-code, which can then be pulled off with any mobile phone. You can either print this on the tickets when they are created or make small stickers containing the ticket ID.

Ensuring the flow of work is the main task at Kanban and there are several ways to measure how fast and well the current flows. But what determines "good and fast"? A simple graph can help by recording the time on one axis and the number of completed tasks on the other. This graphic is also called the Cumulative Task Flow. Even better, all tickets should be calculated according to their status (To-Do, Doing, Done). Then you get a pretty good overview of how the flow actually is. The ideal situation would be if all curves were flat and slowly tipped downwards over time. Finally, there are three scenarios:

a. The curves point upwards: There are too many tickets at the same time

b. The curve is flat: The project runs according to your plan

   c. The curve points downwards: You have some free capacity, which can mean that you either have too few tasks in the process or your team is working faster

At the beginning it will be normal for the curves to change a bit; especially at the beginning you will have a lot of tickets in the backlog. This chart will only give you a general overview. Equally important are the changes in the tickets that are in progress. This is often referred to as cycle time: How long does a job take and how much time has been estimated for it? If each ticket gets a time limit, you can see in this chart if the work takes too long or if your time limits were wrong. You can also measure how long it takes for a request to be processed in its entirety, from backlog to done.

Another important graphic shows the blocked tasks and how they are resolved. A task can be blocked for various reasons: Further resources are missing; a change request was received; the employee has become ill. Blocked tickets are removed from the calculation of the maximum number of tickets in process. However, if you have too many blocked tickets, it means that a lot of work is unfinished. If you apply the blocked tickets on a graphic against a timeline, you can see how long they stand still and how long it usually takes for them to be resolved.

Your goal is to have as few blocked tickets as possible because they can often be a hidden bottleneck.

5.2.3 Does Kanban have burndown charts?

One of the most popular tools in the Agile world is the Burndown Charts. They indicate how much work has been done and how much work is still available. Finally, the Burndown Chart shows you how close your project is to the plan in terms of time.

Since Kanban is more process-oriented and has no completion date, there are no real burndown charts. However, you can use a few tricks to see if the work is done fast enough. The overview already gives you an overview of how the work goes, but with a burndown chart you want a zero at the end, i.e. the curve runs in the direction of the X-axis. You can do this by splitting a column into two columns: Each ticket is first in the left column and is divided into its components: These can be sub-tickets, certain tests, whatever. Whenever one of these elements is completed, it is moved to the right column. At the end, the left column is empty and you have a value of 0, which you can display in a graph.

Such tricks are mainly used with Scrumban, a hybrid of Scrum and Kanban. Always remember that in Kanban the flow of work is the center of attention and not the end of it. Burndown charts should therefore only be a means to see if the project is finished on time, but not if it is going well at the moment.

Good tracking will only be possible with software. You will have to try to convert the board into data. This can be done, for example, by using the QR codes mentioned above.

5.3 Why pull is so important and must be defined

Kanban and other lean management systems live on the pull principle. This means that raw materials are produced on demand, i.e. they are only demanded when they run out in the work process. In software development, these raw materials are the requirements and product descriptions. These are only brought into the work and development process if the necessary capacities are available. A second important step is the decision that a product is ready and can be delivered. In this case, the delivery warehouse pulls the products to it and makes room in the work-in-progress process again.

When software is designed, there is above all a large catalogue of requirements. The customer has written down what he expects from the software, the business and product managers have formulated it in such a way that it can be divided into development steps, and the programmers in turn divide it into parts that can be written together or separately in codes.

A classic Kanban board in software development looks like this:

To-Do	Design	Development	Testing	Deliver

The To-Do column contains the tasks that designers, developers or testers can get. Once they have taken an element, it is transferred to the corresponding columns and usually given its name. All columns must have a rule about the maximum number of tasks that can be done simultaneously. For a smaller company, however, you should also have a rule that limits the maximum number of tickets in progress for one person because in Kanban it is possible that someone interrupts a job (which must be clearly noted on the board). If this person has too many other jobs, there may be a delay that can affect the entire development.

When a design is done, a code written, or a product tested, it is marked "finished" or "done". And then nothing happens until someone gets this ticket and delivers it. This is the big difference between Kanban and other systems. Something is completed and marked as such, but it is not pushed further but has to be fetched. In this way, Kanban ensures that only as much work is in progress as is actually needed.

In software development, the designer gets the elements from the to-do list, the developer gets the finished elements from the designer area and the tester gets the finished products. So you always have an overview of the flow in production and can see at a glance which columns are filled (which means stagnation) or empty (which is also a problem because the employees don't get any work).

To keep track of what work is done within an area, you can split the Design, Development, and Testing columns into Doing and Done, and in this case the ticket will be moved to the Done area. But this is less a part of the workflow than a way to keep the board organized.

If your company and your team have never worked with Agile before, you will need to help get the pull system up and running at the beginning. Most employees were used to being assigned the work, now they have to get it on their own. The morning meeting at the Kanban Board can also help to solve this problem by discussing together who takes care of which work.

With the introduction of Kanban, you will only have one board in a smaller team, but when it comes to bringing Kanban to a larger operation, you will need to plan something first. The ADACOR Group was faced with the task of using Kanban but first had to think about how it could be organized. This was not about a project but about basically using Kanban as task management. This meant, however, because of the many tasks, that one had to set up at least one board per department. The company described in their blog how it could help to automate certain parts in Kanban:

A developer should always check for certain standards after completion of the programming and then hand over the task to another employee for testing.

In order to fulfill this requirement, we have designed a column rule system in several development meetings, in which the column of a board can be provided with configurable rules that trigger defined actions as soon as a task is moved into or out of the corresponding column. You can choose from a set of predefined rules and then specify for which column the rule should apply and whether it should be applied to incoming or outgoing tasks or only to certain task types.

The predefined rules include, e.g.:

Forcing a Change of Employee

Sending an Info-Mail (Recipient configurable)

Force a comment

Confirm a checklist (checklist items configurable)

Due to the wealth of features and the corresponding complexity, we let all considerations and concepts rest for a few days after each concept meeting and talked about them daily in the team. At the next concept meeting, the topic was discussed again until we agreed that we had developed a good approach.[5]

---

[5] Krack, S. (2013): Erfahrungsbericht einer Kanban-Implementierung. URL: https://blog.adacor.com/erfahrungsbericht-kanban-implementierung_874.html [as of: 31-07-2018]

5.4 Service-classes and -types

If you have now defined the basic structure for your board and added the first elements to the to-do list, you will notice that it quickly becomes confusing. Even the separation between design, development and testing is not enough. Two more elements are needed: service classes and service types.

Classes are descriptions of when and why something needs to be edited. You can also see this as priorities, but they have a certain basis. This is often the cost of delay. What is meant by that is: What are the costs if this element is not processed? You don't have to write these costs down in euros and cents, it's more about being aware of the effects a certain element has.

The **service classes** can be:

- Urgent processing

- Must be processed by...

- Express processing

- Costs not (yet) representable

An online shop can serve as an example: If a ticket was opened that says that the load on the web server is too high then the highest priority is given because the server might fail or become too slow. Urgent processing is called for here.

For example, a ticket can be the development of a static page for a summer offer: This page must then logically be ready by the summer and gets a time-defined service class.

Sometimes, despite the best planning, a small part can be missing, for example two fields of an order form. Since the non-editing (and thus the non-activation) of the order form can cause high costs, it is more favorable to carry out this work with an express processing. However, you must make sure that there are not too many elements in this class.

The costs that are not yet known may be elements that may cause high costs, but you don't know if and when: An example might be that there may be changes to the cloud provider, but you can't tell yet how they will affect your product.

The last and most used class is Normal or Standard, which is used for non-urgent day work.

Note: You should set up a rule about how many elements of the different service classes there can be at the same time, similar to the rule that limits the elements in the different work-in-progress columns. To make it a little easier for you to subdivide the work, there are service types.

The service types are about defining the type of work a little more precisely. Let's say a part of the product is tested and the test is negative. Then it needs to be reworked and goes back to the to-do list: But how do the employees know it's a repair? This is where service types come into play.

The **common types** are:

- **Feature**

- **Change**

- **Bug**

And with these service types, you can also impose restrictions; for example, you can only design, develop and test 10 features at a time or you only have five bugs in work in progress. These restrictions are often used as swimlanes.

A good rule at Kanban is: "Don't put more on your plate than you can eat."[6] This is exactly what many of the rules are for, which above all restrict work. It is too easy to write down all ideas and jobs on a board and then wait to see if someone gets the work. At Porsche, Kanban was introduced to IT. To avoid an overflow right at the beginning (the input trap), there was a classic backlog. This is managed by a team that removes new elements on a weekly basis and puts them on the board. This is usually done according to criteria such as urgency or time constraints. This allows Porsche employees to control the entire amount of work quite well. Change requests are an exception: They are entered directly on the board, as to-do, and are then prioritized in the morning meetings.

At Porsche, tasks are referred to as tickets that employees pick up. The process is as follows:

Each task (ticket) moves on the board from left to right and passes through the columns work preparation, implementation, optional integration, and internal or external acceptance, one after the other,

---

[6] Bonrad, O. (2017): Mit Kanban das Chaos beherrschen: unsere Erfahrungen bis heute. URL: https://www.porscheinformatik.at/mit-kanban-das-chaos-beherrschen-unsere-erfahrungen-bis-heute/ [as of: 20-07-2018]

until it is completed. This process - as the analysis has shown - is suitable for practically all our activities.

The ticket contains, among other things, the working title, customer order or internal improvement, and has space for colored markings. Colored dots represent the different teams involved in the ticket. Depending on the team, there are also markers for individual employees and - very importantly - space for a blocker. The blocker stands out visually and contains brief information as to why the ticket cannot be processed any further, i.e. what exactly (as an external cause outside the work area) blocks the ticket.

The tickets move from left to right but are processed from right to left. Thus, work in progress is finished before a new one is started. [7]

The colour design in particular enabled the carmakers to install additional levels that the employees could better allocate to the tasks.

---

[7] Bonrad, O. (2017): Mit Kanban das Chaos beherrschen: unsere Erfahrungen bis heute. URL: https://www.porscheinformatik.at/mit-kanban-das-chaos-beherrschen-unsere-erfahrungen-bis-heute/ [as of: 20-07-2018]

5.5 Kanban meetings

No project management can do without regular meetings. Even if this is Lean Management, which is supposed to reduce the bureaucratic water head and accelerate the process, you will have to sit down again and again to discuss the progress of the process and project.

Most important is the morning meeting, which roughly corresponds to the Daily Scrum. Here all participants meet every morning at the Kanban Board and discuss the most important tasks for the day. It's about everyone having the same information and deciding quickly and effectively how to keep the process flowing. For example, the person responsible for filling the work-in-progress column can give hints as to what has priority and why. Or the delivery manager can ask not to deliver all work at the same time because otherwise they cannot be accepted quickly enough by customers. These morning meetings should last no longer than 15 minutes and take place as early as possible, at the beginning of the working day if possible.

At Porsche, the 15-minute rule has been adhered to and experience has been positive, says Oliver Bonrad, who is a member of the Porsche Server

Client Operation team. Above all, communication between the departments and within the team have been improved by the tightly conducted meetings. The unnecessary and tedious e-mail traffic has also been significantly reduced: If there was a problem, they sat down and found a solution. This was done faster and with better quality than before. Another advantage was that the meetings were also attended by employees who were not always involved in the direct work. But they got a better understanding of how the Porsche IT staff work, which greatly improved the working atmosphere.

5.6 Replenishment meeting

One of the core elements of Kanban is that the system ensures smooth replenishment. In the industry this is done with simple cards: Once a container has reached a certain minimum quantity, a card is removed and a refill is ordered. This ensures that sufficient raw materials are always available. This is somewhat more difficult in software development. You don't really have a container with zeros and ones from which codes are written. Instead you have the requirements and the descriptions of the products. However, these are not automatically added but must be prioritized. This process is one of Kanban's weaknesses in software development because it is the one that is most likely to slow down the flow. It is therefore all the more important that in the replenishment meetings it is made clear according to which rules[8] new tasks are pushed into the work process or how the developers can extract these tasks. The replenishment meetings can take place weekly or every two weeks, usually depending on the progress of the project.

---

[8] Singh, M. (2017): 7 Factors for running an effective Kanban Replenishment Meeting. URL: https://www.digite.com/blog/kanban-replenishment-meeting/amp/ [as of: 02-08-2018]

Purpose

Everyone involved should understand why this meeting exists, why they are attending it, and what is expected of them. It's not about discussing the content of tasks but about organizing them so that it's clear which ones can be taken and edited when. It's all about what's best for the workflow and getting the product ahead, rather than the actual features of a particular task—even if they have an impact on priority. Most of the time it's done very quickly by the team, but be prepared that if stakeholders are involved, it can be a bit longer. Then try to introduce a time limit.

Criteria

In order to prevent discussions, you should formulate clear criteria according to which tasks can be taken from the to-do list. This can sometimes lead to conflicts between the various participants because everyone considers their tasks to be particularly urgent. Therefore the following criteria can help you to bring order into chaos:

Risk

What is the risk if the task is not done? What processes are involved if it has no priority?

Cost of delay

If a task is not completed immediately, this can drive up costs, among other things. Even if this is a well-known criterion, you will sometimes have problems presenting the costs as figures. For example, a feedback form may be important, but what costs will it incur if it remains a little late? Often you will have to estimate here or check whether the individual product parts have already been quantified in the project plan.

Dependencies

This is often a powerful argument for a high priority: If other product parts are dependent on it and would have to wait if they were not processed. You can also call a risk a block risk here and use a scale from 1 to 5: 5 stands for the fact that it certainly brings with it blockages. Which criteria you apply always depends on the project and the team. However, you should make sure that all these criteria are known and accepted.

Workflow

In the replenishment meetings you can also explain – especially at the beginning – how the workflow is guaranteed; after all, this is a core element at Kanban. It must be clear to everybody that the work is taken out as soon as possible, as soon as capacities have become available, but also goes into the right channels, for example when swimlanes are used. With Kanban it is not so important who gets the work but above all that it gets it. Often there can also be new insights at the replenishment meetings, which can lead, for example, to the fact that you have to open a new board because a process is better outsourced or that you need new swimlanes because a certain team should not be separated.

5.7 Delivery meeting

This is where customers come in. This meeting, which can take place on a monthly basis, is about what the customer wants delivered and at what intervals. Because as nice as it is that Kanban, when it runs optimally, constantly delivers new finished product parts, it can be overwhelming for the customer. At the delivery meetings you will bring the team and the customer together and you will discuss which elements the customer expects next but also whether he is able to accept them accordingly. Essentially, it is about preventing the customer from being overwhelmed with products, but at the same time it is also about preventing products from not being delivered because of this and from being left in the exit.

While the monthly meeting is more of a planning meeting, it should also be used to discuss which products will be delivered on that day and whether they match the planning. If developers know what to ship, they can also better decide which parts to ship that day.

5.8 Service meeting

Above all, Kanban wants to satisfy its customers. Software companies tend to isolate themselves and get to work according to an assumed project plan and reduce customer contact to delivering finished work. A service meeting is about evaluating whether the customer is satisfied with the process, the products delivered so far, and the way they are treated. These meetings can be held internally. The easiest way is to take the most recently delivered work and discuss with the team how the customer received it but also whether it was good enough to be presented to the customer at all. It's also about what the client gives in feedback, but it's also about whether everyone in the team understands what the client wants and is guided by it. So it can happen that a developer starts to develop a form because he likes to do it, but the customer needs another functionality more urgently.

At these meetings, we also discuss how to deal with complaints and how the customer reacted to them. Something will always go wrong; it is important that you are able to solve the problem together with the customer and to give him the feeling that he is in good hands with you and your team even in case of difficulties.

5.9 Risk meetings

Because even the best plan can go wrong and there are always events that can disturb a Kanban system, you should constantly prepare yourself for existing risks. In the risk meetings it is therefore discussed whether such risks are already coming but also which can arise and what influence they can have.

A serious risk can be, for example, that there will be a traffic jam of finished work because the customer suddenly lacks the resources to accept the work. This can (and will) influence your flow considerably. If you have thought about the risks before, you are better able to manage them.

Already during the planning of the whole project you should have made an exact risk analysis, so that with the risk meetings only one has to look at whether these have occurred or how high the probability is that they will occur.

But you can also use the risk meetings as an opportunity to learn from mistakes you have made. They are the right place to analyse mistakes and develop ideas together on how such mistakes can be avoided in the future.

A risk meeting can be held once a month or even when you have a problem to solve that was previously unknown. In addition, you can, of course, announce in the morning meetings what mistakes have happened, what you have learned from them, and how you want to avoid them.

Especially in software development, mistakes can happen again and again, the effects of which may only become visible later. So your team members should prepare themselves for bugs; you can do regular short workshops in which the main thing is to understand the nature of the bug and see it as part of the workflow. Participants must learn that mistakes arise and are not a problem as long as they are transparent and processed.

5.10 Strategy meetings

These meetings are only held if there is a reason to change the previous strategy. It is not so much a question of whether the Kanban process has problems but of the product itself. Let's assume that you are currently developing software that makes it easier to calculate and manage payroll tax. Suddenly the legislator comes up with the idea of introducing new calculation bases. Now you have to strategically realign your product, for example from "The simplest income tax calculator" to "The most current income tax calculator", which of course also includes the quick adaptation to the new law.

Another reason could be that a competitor suddenly appears who develops a similar product. Now it is a matter of finding a new orientation, a new market, being faster or taking up the fight. Whatever solution you are considering, you have to think about the strategy.

After some time, Porsche realized that Kanban worked very well, but it needed to be fine-tuned further. Some columns that more precisely defined a completed job were abolished, with the result that employees had more space to group tasks. Another idea that came up was not only to assign a Swimlane to a service team but also to extend it to other teams. Such experiments are good and important at Kanban, and you should also be flexible enough to adapt the system constantly. Exactly these adjustments can be addressed in the strategy meetings. The carmaker's IT specialists had also set up a parking lot for tickets that were either further in the future or required the cooperation of third parties that were not yet available. The problem with these tickets was that they blocked the amount of work in progress without anyone being able to process them. However, you will have to make sure that the tickets you parked there are not forgotten.

Important requirements for meetings

From Scrum you can learn that meetings should be time-boxed, i.e. have an exact and usually tight time schedule. The morning meeting should not last longer than 15 minutes. All other meetings should not exceed 30 minutes. Risk and strategy meetings can be an exception. Every meeting, except the morning meeting, must have an agenda that is made available to participants in a timely manner. Each participant is asked in advance to develop ideas about what to talk about.

The above list includes a lot of meetings, and some people are now thinking about the countless meetings they have in project teams, especially in large organizations. In Kanban, there is no fixed rule as to when a meeting should take place (except for the morning meeting), and so Kanban meetings are event-based. If there is a reason to sit down, it is done. If everything goes well, you don't have to meet.

Kanban expert David Anderson called these meetings the seven cadences of Kanban but at the same time pointed out that you should keep them in mind rather than sending Outlook invitations every day. Meanwhile, some companies have also limited morning meetings to three times a week because there was simply not enough to discuss and time was better spent on current work.

5.11 Responsibilities in Kanban

In contrast to Scrum, where roles are very important, Kanban's accountability is less strict. However, this does not mean that anarchy prevails here. In practice at least three roles have been established, which can be found in most Kanban projects.

5.11.1 Project manager

The project manager is responsible for ensuring that Kanban runs, that the flow is available and that he only has to intervene when there are certain problems. He has to make sure that all necessary resources are available, especially concerning the personnel. It can also be his responsibility if Kanban has to be extended, for example to suppliers or external service providers. In software development, for example, this can be the case if certain areas are programmed externally. These are usually special tasks such as artificial intelligence or virtual reality. Nevertheless, they must be integrated into the Kanban process and it is the project manager's task to ensure this. Like everything at Kanban, this is done together with the team.

Often the project manager has to satisfy the stakeholders. He maintains contact with customers, especially at management level, or with department heads when a project is carried out within an organization. There is usually a monthly meeting to discuss progress. While industrial Kanban projects are all about whether everything is running smoothly, software projects will be about how far you are with completion.

5.11.2 Service request manager

The main task of the Service Request Manager is to understand the customer's interests and to present their wishes in the Kanban flow. In concrete terms, this means ensuring that the work being done has the highest priority and is best suited to achieving progress. You can also call him a Product Manager or Operations Manager. Role names are not important in Kanban, but you will need someone to ensure that the work is distributed and have an overview of whether, for example, new work is sufficiently defined. If, for example, credit cards are a condition in the conception phase for taxi software, then it must also be ensured that one has the rights to use and a corresponding agreement exists for the use of the interface of the respective card service.

5.11.3 Delivery request manager

The Delivery Request Manager works closely with the project manager and the Service Request Manager but focuses on the completed parts of the software. His task is to deliver these finished elements to the customer and have them accepted by the customer. He is also usually the person who, together with the project manager, leads the Kanban meetings and plans the delivery of finished work. In projects where it is important to get work finished as quickly as possible, he will be the flow master who ensures flow from the delivery side. Where it is more important that the right elements are processed first, the Service Request Manager will take over.

6. Tools to use Kanban

To use Kanban over one software, you can use different software solutions. Below you will find a selection, which should mainly show the bandwidth, in which there are offers. Software solutions are often tailored to specific industries, such as the software industry or logistics. There is no consensus on whether you should use a traditional board or software at Kanban. The board is always appropriate when the teams are small and everyone has access to the board at all times. The more complex the work becomes, the more likely you are to want to use software. A big advantage of the programs is that they can create reports very quickly. Even though Kanban per se provides a good overview of the progress of the project, software analysis methods allow you to see even better if and where there are discrepancies.

6.1 Trello

Trello is one of the simplest solutions but one that is ideal for beginners. Behind it is an online service that allows you to create and configure your own boards. You can start with three columns "To Do - Doing - Done" and adjust the whole thing piece by piece. For example, you can create a board with which you want to plan the actual board and conveniently jump back and forth between the two boards.

Even though Trello doesn't see itself as a Kanban solution, it has everything you need for Kanban. For example, you can reduce the number of tickets in a column (there is no menu for that, you just have to put the number corresponding to the maximum in square brackets, for example Testing [5]. If there are more than five test tickets, the column turns red). These columns are called trello lists; you can create as many lists as you want, they are displayed horizontally one after the other. The tasks or tickets in Trello are called Cards. You can add a date to these cards, a color; you can make an employee responsible for them (or several) and you can also create subtasks. Once a task is completed, it is simply dragged and dropped into the next column.

The disadvantage with Trello is that the mobile version doesn't give you a good overview. It shows you your tasks, but you can't capture the flow in Kanban well. The more columns, the more difficult it becomes, also because the cards are very text-heavy. And like all online-based systems you have to pay extra for each employee.

But Trello is very intuitive to use and doesn't require a long introductory phase or much training.

6.2 Leankit

Leankit is very popular, particularly because the company has made it its business to pass on and spread the knowledge about Kanban. In the company's blog you will find excellent articles about Kanban and project management. The name says that they try to provide tools for Lean Production and Agile Development. If Trello is for the beginner, then Leankit is used by large companies and tries to integrate different Lean methods. It can be used for Kanban as well as for Scrum. The focus is on visibility, cards are colored throughout. The company itself says, "Our products are based on the human preference for visual information." With Leankit you can see at a glance how your project is running and then dive into the details. What's especially nice are the built-in statistics. You can have all data displayed in an excellent visual format and thus see even better where your project stands at the moment and where there are problems. Because LeanKit is primarily aimed at companies, there is an enterprise version that is almost infinitely scalable. Of course Leankit is also available as an app. On an iPad it's clearer than on a smartphone but still clearer than Trello.

6.3 Jira Software

This project management has been written especially for software developers who want agile methods but also want to work together online. It comes from <u>Atlassian</u>, which also distributes Trello. But Jira is on a much more professional level than Trello. The basis here are story cards, which contain all essential information and also show what makes them somewhat text-heavy. By clicking on one of the cards you can call up or insert further information. The boards at Jira are very easy to create. The program even helps you to develop a board according to your wishes. It's just as easy to add work-in-progress limits, which not only show that a limit has been reached but also reject new entries. Jira is very adaptable and can be easily scaled. It spits out a graphic about the workflow so you can see how well your project is performing, but it also has other statistics tools at hand. Another advantage is that it also has Scrum functions built in if you develop your project with Scrum and Kanban. For the Kanban purists the visual clarity is missing here with the boards, the columns are not neatly separated, the stories look too similar. More color would be desirable here. If you set up Jira yourself, then you will need some time to understand all the functions. But once the board is set up, teams and staff can get started quickly.

6.4 Kanbanize

This software is tailor-made for the Kanban fan. It is available in three versions: Portfolio as an enterprise solution, team for projects and personnel for personal use. The portfolio version gives you a complete overview, especially when it comes to managing multiple projects. Here, too, the visual has been placed before the details and you will see at a glance what is going on in which project without having to know the details right away. In addition, Kanbanize provides you with constantly updated reports on the status of the individual projects—sometimes too many. Nevertheless you can save a lot of time with individualized and automated reports and quickly browse through the status of your projects. The software is also able to link projects together. This can be important if an employee works in two projects and actually has enough work in one project. If there is a limit for tasks per employee as a rule, a warning will be displayed or further tasks for the employee will be blocked. The same applies to the use of other resources.

In the team solution, you can execute a project and see at any time how good the progress is. Here, too, great importance has been attached to the visual design and overview. What your employees and you will be happy about is that reports are generated automatically. If you should have to report to your boss, Kanbanize will automatically create a status report, depending on which specifications have been made for these reports. As in most Agile environments, Kanbanize is designed for collaboration and transparency. Team members should also be able to see the entire project and not just their individual tasks. Kanbanize is now used by large companies such as the speaker manufacturer Bose and the chemical giant Roche as well as the soccer club Arsenal.

6.5 Kanbantool

The company Share Labs, which specializes in web applications, has provided Kanbantool, a very versatile tool for project management. The Polish company has 25,000 users worldwide, including prominent names such as Pirelli and Cisco.

The software aims to improve efficiency and productivity in the company and its processes. Here, too, the focus is on visualization. Kanban is aimed primarily at large companies, as can be seen from the design of the interface, which is very clear and sober. Start-ups looking for playful solutions are more likely to be deterred here. But this has no influence on the functionality; Kanbantool offers everything a project manager's heart desires. It is perfectly suited to handle even very large projects and large quantities of tasks and makes it easy for employees to work together. The developers have put a lot of emphasis on data analysis, and you can have a separate report output for almost every process. The service is cloud-based, but there is also a solution that you can install on your own server. The cost is $5 per user per month for the Team solution and $9 per user per month for the Enterprise solution. This puts you in the middle price segment for such solutions.

6.6 Microsoft Surface Hub

A technological compromise solution is the Microsoft Surface Hub. This is a very large touch screen that can be mounted on the wall or simply placed on a stand. The advantage is that you have a board that is quite mobile, offers a visual representation for everyone and has all the data electronically prepared. The disadvantage is that the device currently only works with Microsoft certified apps. However, these are very strongly designed for collaboration, project management and meetings, so that you can also use them to manage a Kanban project. It is helpful that it has a touch screen, which can simulate the haptic experience of the real board at least a little bit. But the board isn't cheap: for the 83-inch screen you have to pay a proud 22,000 euros.

7. Other uses for Kanban

7.1 How to organize your warehouse with Kanban

Kanban can be used not only in production according to its original meaning or in software development as an agile environment, but also in material management, for example in a hospital group. A study[9] by the Reliant Medical Group has shown how this works…

In a hospital it is very important to be supplied with medication but also with other materials such as bandages, syringes and catheters. The only problem is that medicines have a sell-by date that must be adhered to exactly, and other materials are sometimes consumed more quickly than they are delivered later but are also stored in a warehouse for too long. Many of Reliant's clinics are subdivided into departments, such as Pediatrics and Orthopaedics, and each has its own small warehouse. So far, replenishments have been delivered once a week,

---

[9] Chung-Chuen-Yeung (2012): Implementing a Kanban Replenishment System at Reliant Medical Group. URL: https://web.wpi.edu/Pubs/E-project/Available/E-project-042512-135450/unrestricted/KanbanImplementation.pdf [as of: 23-07-2018]

based on the assessments of the warehouse staff. The stock was recorded manually, which has led to many errors.

As an improvement, Kanban cards were introduced, which followed a precise labeling rule: a serial number, the name, whether it has to be ordered internally or externally, the unit in which it is delivered (box, rolls, etc.), where it can be found in the warehouse (shelf number), when a new order is required, and what the minimum quantity is. These cards were placed in each box. In addition, all materials were divided into two boxes. If one was empty, the Kanban card was removed and reordered, while the second box ensured that sufficient material was available until delivery.

7.2 How to organize your life with Kanban

Today it is common that, apart from work and family, there are many other obligations that cost a lot of time but also need organisation. Kanban can help to organize your life and reduce stress on a very simplified level. It can also help within a family to organise housework, plan holidays and monitor finances.

All you need is a board with Post-Its or other cards that have a column marked "To do", a column marked "In work" and a column marked "Done". For example, a job could be lawn mowing. Let's say that's your job. Then take the card with the inscription "Mowing the lawn" and paste it into the "In progress" area. Then you start mowing the lawn. When you are finished, mark the card, for example with a green hook sticker. Another member of the family can then see if the garden has been mowed properly and move the card to the "Done" area. What sounds so complicated can be a lot of fun in a family, especially if all family members have to do some work and, for example, the children have to accept the work of their parents as "Done". In this way they learn to take responsibility but also that you trust them and that you have to work together with others.

8. Summary

Kanban is an established method in industrial production and also in software development to save material, time and human resources during the production or development of a product. Whenever you have a project that needs to be managed and executed as efficiently as possible, Kanban can be the right solution.

One of the big advantages of Kanban is that it can grow with a company or a project. You can start with three columns and end up with a three-meter-long board with 10 swimlanes and 7 different columns for work-in-progress. This makes Kanban itself a work in progress and will change over the course of the project. Kanban is only a method to make the workflow more efficient, not an end in itself. If at some point you find that Kanban can no longer achieve the goals it is supposed to achieve, then you should look for another solution.

Especially in software development it has been shown that mixed approaches like Scrumban work better because they are more suitable to reflect the essence of software development. The sprints in particular can speed up the workflow considerably, even if they are not intended in Kanban.

In order for Kanban to be successful, you should talk to all participants at the beginning about what you expect and what they expect. A good cooperation based on a common understanding of what you want to create together (and how) is the cornerstone for a successful Kanban project.

The book is intended to give you an overview and an introduction to the world of Kanban. With what you have learned, you should be able to manage small and medium-sized projects with Kanban; but if a project gets too big or if you don't have the time to take care of the introduction yourself, you should seek advice and help from outside. Just as there are consultants at Scrum today, some have specialized in Kanban and can help to implement Kanban in a company. Such consulting does not come for free, but especially at Kanban it has been shown that you can save a lot of money by making the workflow as efficient and fast as possible.

Yours
Franz Millweber

Bibliography

Bonrad, O. (2017): Mit Kanban das Chaos beherrschen: unsere Erfahrungen bis heute. URL: https://www.porscheinformatik.at/mit-kanban-das-chaos-beherrschen-unsere-erfahrungen-bis-heute/ [as of: 20-07-2018]

Chung-Chuen-Yeung (2012): Implementing a Kanban Replenishment System at Reliant Medical Group. URL: https://web.wpi.edu/Pubs/E-project/Available/E-project-042512-135450/unrestricted/KanbanImplementation.pdf [as of: 23-07-2018]

Krack, S. (2013): Erfahrungsbericht einer Kanban-Implementierung. URL: https://blog.adacor.com/erfahrungsbericht-kanban-implementierung_874.html [as of: 31-07-2018]

Laptick, S. (2016): How & Why to Use the Kanban Methodology for Software Development.URL; https://www.sitepoint.com/how-why-to-use-the-kanban-methodology-for-software-development/ [as of: 22-07-2018]

Leankit Inc.: 10 Kanban Board Example. URL: https://leankit.com/learn/kanban/kanban-board-examples-for-development-and-operations [as of: 05-08-2018]

Leopold, K. (2017): Flight Level: The Organizational Improvement Levels. URL: https://www.leanability.com/en/blog-en/2017/04/flight-levels-the-organizational-improvement-levels [as of: 10-08-2018]

Singh, M. (2017): 7 Factors for running an effective Kanban Replenishment Meeting. URL: https://www.digite.com/blog/kanban-replenishment-meeting/amp/ [as of: 02-08-2018]

Weigand: Die Kanban Methode in der Praxis. URL: https://www.weigang.de/de/themenwelt/methoden/kanban/kanban-anwendungsbeispiel [as of: 20-08-2018]